the
story
of old glory

Dedicated to the Boy Scouts of America
Cub Scouts, Boy Scouts and Explorers

The Story of Old Glory

Author
John R. Manning

Edited by
Norris J. Nelson

Critically reviewed by
THE FLAG RESEARCH CENTER
17 Farmcrest Avenue, Lexington, Mass. 02173

Norman Rockwell painting page 3
is reproduced by permission of and copyrighted by Brown & Bigelow,
a division of Standard Packaging Corporation
and permission of the National Council,
Boy Scouts of America.

State Flag illustrations courtesy Dettra Flag Company, Inc.

Published by
THE CONTINUING EDUCATION INSTITUTE, INC.
4350 East Camelback Rd., Phoenix, Arizona 85018

The Continuing Education Institute, inc

4350 E. CAMELBACK ROAD · PHOENIX, ARIZONA 85018 · (602) 959-7080

To a Friend of Scouting

Ever since Scouting began, over 61 years ago, Boy Scouts have been taught respect for Old Glory and to obey the rules, regulations and laws governing its dignity.

Love and respect of our flag has always been a fundamental principal and law of Scouting.

This edition of The Story of Old Glory, published by The Continuing Education Institute exclusively for the Boy Scouts of America will be used by many Scout Troops, Cub Packs and Explorers Posts as a fund raising project.

The purchase of this copy of The Story of Old Glory indicates that you, or the friend that gave it to you, has been a "Good Scout" and has helped support a local Boy Scout organization.

We thank you for your support.

Norris J. Nelson
Editor and Publisher

GROWTH OF A LEADER
by Norman Rockwell 1966

I am Old Glory

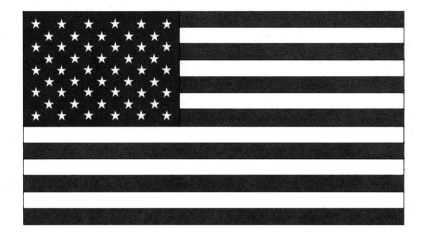

    For almost 200 years I have been the banner of hope and freedom for generation after generation of Americans. Born amid the first flames of America's fight for freedom, I am the symbol of a country that has grown from a little group of thirteen colonies to a united nation of fifty sovereign states. Planted firmly on a high pinnacle of American faith, my gently fluttering folds have proved an inspiration to untold millions. Men have followed me into battle with unwavering courage. They have looked upon me as a symbol of national unity. They have prayed that they and their fellow citizens might continue to enjoy the life, liberty and pursuit of happiness which have been granted to every American as the heritage of free men. So long as men love liberty more than life itself, so long as they treasure the priceless privileges bought with the blood of our forefathers, so long as the principles of truth, justice and charity for all remain deeply rooted in human hearts, I shall continue to be the enduring banner of the United States of America.

Pledge of Allegiance

*"I pledge allegiance to the Flag of
the United States of America and
to the Republic for which it stands,
one Nation under God, indivisible,
with liberty and justice for all."*

This latest wording of the pledge to our flag was developed from
the original which was drawn up in August, 1892, in the Boston offices
of Youth's Companion, a popular young people's magazine of the time.
It was adopted by Congress in 1942.

The author of the original pledge of allegiance to the flag was
Francis Bellamy, who was born in Mount Morris, N.Y., May 12, 1855,
and died on August 28, 1931.

The American's Creed

*Adopted by the United States House
of Representative on April 3, 1918*

I believe in the United States of America as a Government of the people, by the people, for the people; whose just powers are derived from the consent of the governed; a democracy in a republic; a sovereign Nation of many sovereign States; a perfect union, one and inseparable; established upon those principles of freedom, equality, justice and humanity for which American patriots sacrificed their lives and fortunes. I therefore believe it is my duty to my country to love it; to support its Constitution; to obey its laws, to respect its flag, and to defend it against all enemies.

The World's First Flags

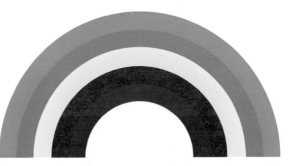

Flags symbolize the noble aspirations and glorious achievements of the human race. They epitomize the romance of history. They incarnate the chivalry of the ages.

The mythical origin of flags is recorded in Genesis. After the Flood, Jehovah made a covenant with man, promising that never again would He send the waters to cover the face of the earth and destroy all flesh. He unfurled the first flag — the multihued banner of the rainbow — which He set in the clouds as a symbol of security and an assurance to all future generations of His watchful care. Since that day, man has employed his earthly banners as emblems of faith, hope, and high resolve.

Centuries before Christ, flags of one kind or another were carried by fighting men. A number of years ago in Northern India, Sir John Marshall, head of the archeological service of the government of India, discovered two abandoned cities: one at a site now called Mohenjo-Daro, the other at Harappa. These cities are believed to have thrived about 3,500 B.C. and were in close contact with the earliest civilizations of Babylonia. Among the objects found in the former city was a seal used to sign documents and showing a procession of seven men carrying square standards held aloft on poles like modern flags. These ancient flags were made not of cloth but were rigid solids like boards.

In ancient Egypt, objects ranging from sacred animals to tablets bearing a king's name were borne into battle and carried on ships at the top of a staff. In Persia an eagle was carried on the end of a lance, and in early Greece a piece of armor borne on a spear served as a standard. The Romans guarded their flags in temples with religious veneration, and Roman generals sometimes had the standard thrown into the enemy's ranks, knowing that their soldiers would fight furiously to recover what to them was one of the most sacred things on earth. Later in the Middle Ages, flags were influenced by the development of heraldry and personal coats of arms.

Flags That Have Flown Over North America

THE VIKING FLAG

The Viking Black Raven

For the Norse explorers sailing the "Sea of Darkness" during the 11th Century, the black raven became a symbol of hope during months of doubt and perplexity. These Vikings during their voyages learned to depend upon the raven to lead them to land. It was with the help of this faithful bird that Leif Ericsson and his stalwart crew reached the southernmost tip of Greenland and finally dropped anchor somewhere on the coast of North America. His and other Norse expeditions may have carried the Raven flag with them, since that banner had been used by the Vikings for hundreds of years. If so, it was the first European flag in the New World, preceding by five centuries, the Spanish flags carried by Columbus.

THE SPANISH FLAGS

Christopher Columbus, an Italian, was the first explorer to carry a Spanish flag to North America. When he and his crew set foot on the island of San Salvador in the Bermuda group on October 12, 1492, they bore both the official flag of Spain and a special expeditionary banner.

The flag of Spain was an ornate combination of the emblems of Spain's two principal provinces of that time. Castile and Leon. The quartered banner displayed a castle in gold on a red field for Castile and a lion in crimson on a white field for Leon.

The banner of the expedition bore the cross of Christianity on a white field, with the letters F and Y for Ferdinand and Isabella beneath two yellow crowns. Others who explored the New World under the banners of Spain included: Ponce de León, seeker of the Fountain of Youth in Florida in 1512; Cortes, who extended the Spanish domain to Mexico in 1518; DeSoto, who explored the Mississippi Valley from 1539 to 1541; and Coronado, who led a romantic expedition into the deserts of the Southwest.

The first battle between nations to be fought in North America occurred in 1565 when Pedro Menéndez, under the Spanish flag, landed on the St. Johns River in Florida and destroyed the French Huguenot settlement there. Menéndez founded St. Augustine, the oldest city in the United States.

After 1516 the banner of Castile and Leon was replaced by other Spanish flags. One familiar design of that showed the full Spanish coat of arms on a white flag, sometimes with a red diagonal cross added.

After 1785 all the Spanish colonies used a flag of red-yellow-red horizontal stripes, much like the flag of Spain today.

| The Spanish Flag of 1492 | Columbus' Expeditionary Banner | French Flag of the 1500's |

FRENCH FLAGS

The flags of France came to North America in 1534 with Jacques Cartier. He carried the blue banner with gold fleurs-de-lis as he explored the St. Lawrence Gulf and River. He returned again in 1543 and 1545. Other French flags included the white banner of the Bourbons with its powdering of gold fleur-de-lis and the old French national flag — a white cross on a blue field.

In the middle of the 17th century, France claimed sovereignty over all of Canada, the St. Lawrence, the Great Lakes country, and the Mississippi Valley. In 1803 the United States purchased much of this vast area from Napoleon for $15 million, a cost of two-and-a-half cents per acre. The French flag of that era — the famous blue-white-red Tricolor — was then replaced throughout that area by the Stars and Stripes. The influence of both old and new French flags is evident in the banners of several American cities and States.

THE SWEDISH FLAG

Although Sweden acquired no territorial rights in North America, a religious colony of Swedes and Finns established New Sweden on the banks of the Delaware River in 1638. They were overpowered by the Dutch colony in 1655. A group of colonists remained in Delaware County, however, and flourished in agriculture and industry. The blue and gold colors of Sweden are found today in the State flag of Delaware and the city flag of Wilmington.

DUTCH FLAGS

Henry Hudson brought Dutch flags to North America early in the 17th century. Sailing in the *Half Moon* under the financial backing of The United East India Company, Hudson reached New York Bay in 1609 and founded the seaport city of New Amsterdam, today known as New York City.

9

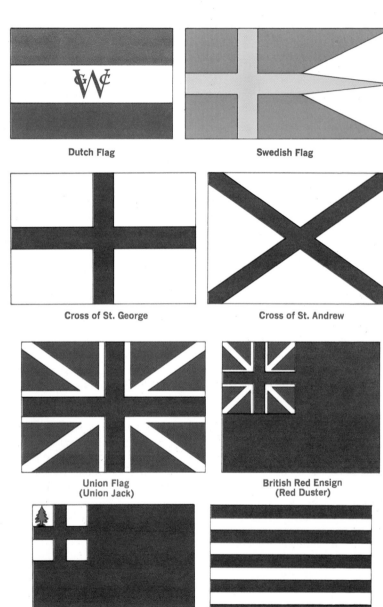

Dutch Flag

Swedish Flag

Cross of St. George

Cross of St. Andrew

Union Flag
(Union Jack)

British Red Ensign
(Red Duster)

Bunker Hill Flag

Sons of Liberty

Hudson's ensign was the flag of the Dutch Republic with its three horizontal stripes (orange, white, and blue). The letters V O C A (standing for *Vereenigte Oost-Indische Compagnie, Amsterdam*) were added in the center of the white stripe. In 1621 when the Chartered West India Company came into control, the letters on the flag were changed to G W C. The orange stripe of all Dutch flags gradually changed to red in the 1600's. Today Hudson's flags are recalled in the blue-white-orange flags flown by New York City, Albany and Hartford.

FLAGS OF BRITAIN

The Cross of St. George and the Cross of St. Andrew were the first British flags brought to North America. John Cabot, sailing westward on a voyage of discovery for King Henry VII of England, bore the Cross of St. George to the shores of Newfoundland. Scottish adventurers brought the Cross of St. Andrew to Nova Scotia at about the same time the English settlements in New England and Virginia were being established.

In 1606 King James I of England, who had been King James VI of Scotland, proclaimed a new flag to represent his rule over both nations. James decreed that the Cross of St. George of England should be combined with the Cross of St. Andrew, Scotland's banner, thus creating what was called the Union Flag or Union Jack.

Joining the two flags is of significance to Americans since it brought together the colors red, white and blue which later became the national colors of the United States of America.

It was the Union Flag which flew at the top mainmasts of the *Susan Constant* and the *Mayflower* when these vessels sailed from England in 1607 and 1620. The flag of St. George appeared at the foremast.

In 1707 Queen Anne established the British Red Ensign, which was sometimes called the Red Duster. The ensign of merchantmen and warships before then had been red with the National Cross of St. George in England or St. Andrew in Scotland in the upper hoist corner. Queen Anne replaced both of these with the Union Flag in the hoist corner, retaining the red field. The British Red Ensign was modified by the American colonists for their own purposes later on. With six white stripes across the red back-ground, it became the Continental Colors — our first national flag.

Other national flags that have flown over territories which are now the United States; Mexican (1823), Russian (1806), California Republic (1846), Republic of Texas (1835), Kingdom of Hawaii (1816).

" . . . *the shot heard round the world.*"

Flags of the American Revolution

When the struggle for independence was first begun in America, there was no common symbol for the 13 colonies. Each local group of men and military force adopted its own standard. Only gradually was the need felt for a united symbol of the new nation.

It is known, however, that Captain Nathaniel Page, one of the minute men from Bedford, Mass., was a flag-bearer for his company at the Battle of Concord, which Emerson described:

> By the rude bridge that arched the flood,
> Their flag to April's breeze unfurled,
> Here once the embattled farmers stood,
> And fired the shot heard round the world.

THE BEDFORD FLAG

Page's standard had a maroon ground and bore an outstretched arm grasping a sword and the motto, inscribed on a scroll in Latin, *Vince aut Morire* — "Conquer or Die." It is the oldest colonial flag in existence. It was made in England sometime after 1660 and now rests in the public library in Bedford, Mass.

BUNKER HILL FLAG (Page 10)

This New England flag with its pine tree emblem flew at the Battle of Bunker Hill on June 17, 1775. It is probably the oldest Colonial flag. It dates back to 1686.

SONS OF LIBERTY (Page 10)

Early revolutionaries, known as the "Sons of Liberty" those patriots who staged the "Boston Tea Party" in December 1773, had their own flag, the "Rebellious Stripes". This nine red and white striped flag represented the nine colonies participating in the Stamp Act Congress. This flag was sometimes used also by colonial merchant ships.

RATTLESNAKE SYMBOL

The rattlesnake, found only in America, is an unusual contribution to America's flag history. Benjamin Franklin first utilized a curved rattlesnake as an emblem for America on the masthead of his famous *Gazette* in 1754.

JOIN, or DIE.

Franklin showed a snake cut into pieces, each of which was identified with the initials of a state. The caption underneath was "Join or Die" — suggesting that the colonies must work together or fail. The rattlesnake was a popular symbol because it was believed that it would strike only when provoked and then only after giving a warning.

DON'T TREAD ON ME FLAG

Commodore Esek Hopkins, America's first Naval Commander-in-Chief was commissioned in the autumn of 1775. His personal rank flag bore a yellow field in the center of which was a coiled rattlesnake, ready to strike if attacked, beneath which was the familiar motto, "Don't Tread on Me." Although this flag is sometimes called the Gadsden flag, Col. Christopher Gadsden had nothing to do with its design or usage. He only had a copy made for the legislature of his home State, South Carolina. Hopkins is also known to have carried on his ship a flag of thirteen stripes without a union or field of stars, but with a rattlesnake undulating diagonally across the stripes and with the same defiant motto.

THE PINE TREE FLAGS

The first local symbol in the American colonies had been the British Red Ensign from which the Puritans cut the cross of St. George. In 1686 when the cross was restored to the flag a small green pine tree was inserted in the upper corner. The pine was important to the commerce of New England. During the next century a pine tree flag of one kind or another was recognized as the distinctive banner of New England.

When the Revolution began, all British symbols were omitted from this flag. Although the Pine tree flags of New England were flown extensively, variations of motto, color, and the position of the pine tree were frequent. While never officially recognized by an act of the Continental Congress, the Pine Tree Flag was in fact employed as the national naval ensign for a time. However, in April, 1776, the Massachusetts legislature officially adopted the Pine Tree Flag in an effort to distinguish American cruisers from the ships of the British merchant marine.

CRESCENT FLAG OF SOUTH CAROLINA

The most famous of the flags used in the South at the beginning of the Revolutionary War was designed in 1775 by Colonel William Moultrie (pronounced MOO-tree), who commanded the Second South Carolina Infantry.

He designed an ensign of blue with white crescent in the upper corner near the staff. The next year the word "liberty" was inscribed on it. This was probably the first distinctive American flag hoisted in the South.

Don't Tread on Me Flag

The Pine Tree Flag

The Moultrie Flag

The Continental Colors

THE CONTINENTAL COLORS

The immediate predecessor to the Stars and Stripes was the Continental Colors, sometimes improperly referred to as the Grand Union or Cambridge Flag. General George Washington ordered it hoisted at Prospect Hill in Charlestown, Mass., on January 1st, 1776, to honor the creation of the Continental Army. History also records that it was flown when Commodore Esek Hopkins' American fleet sailed from Philadelphia in February of the same year.

The flag was designed with the crosses of St. Andrew and St. George in the canton, still indicating the connection with the "mother country." It also displayed thirteen stripes, symbolic of the thirteen colonies. But the Continental Colors was so similar to the British Red Ensign that sometimes the stripes were hoisted without any Union Jack.

The Birth of The Stars and Stripes

It wasn't until the little army of the American Revolution had been bravely and hopefully battling the British forces for two years that some unknown person (perhaps Francis Hopkinson) proposed the establishment of a national flag with stars replacing the Union Jack.

It was on Saturday morning, June 14, 1777, that one of the members of the Marine Committee of the Second Continental Congress introduced and urged the adoption of a resolution which required that:

> "The Flag of the United States be 13 stripes alternate red and white, and the Union be 13 stars white in a blue field representing a new constellation."

This was a memorable day in the history of America. Into being emerged a genuinely American flag, destined to earn the respect of all the powers on earth and become the emblem of more glorious deeds than any other flag in the history of the world.

The Design of the Stars and Stripes

It is probable that General George Washington as Commander in Chief was consulted when the design of our national flag was being discussed and considered.

Many historians have even likened the Stars and Stripes to the coat-of-arms of the Washington family (shown at right) which dates back to Sulgrave Manor, England, 1539.

It is true that the Washington arms bear three red stars and two red stripes on a white field, but it is very unlikely that the modest Washington would have allowed his family heraldry to be used by the new nation.

Moreover, we know that flags bearing only stripes (nine or thirteen) had been used as much as a decade before the Revolution. They were the symbols of young Revolutionaries, particularly the Sons of Liberty. It was simple to modify the British Red Ensign by adding six white stripes across its red field. The result symbolized both the thirteen colonies and their links to the mother country, which had not yet been broken.

Several suggestions had been made concerning the origin of the stars. Possibly they derive from the stars found on certain old Rhode Island military colors and seals. If, as some historians have suggested, the stars come from the city seal of Portsmouth, then we can trace them back to Portsmouth, England. That city obtained its starred coat of arms from King Richard I in 1194. He in turn had found the symbol in the East where it had long represented heavenly aspiration and sovereignty.

During America's first decades both the stars and the stripes were used as symbols of the national union. The eagle, made part of our national coat of arms in 1782, also was a popular emblem. We do not know the full story behind these symbols, although new evidence continues to be found.

Making of the First Stars and Stripes

While popular legend bestows the honor of making the first Stars and Stripes upon Mrs. Betsy Ross, most historians doubt that she made it. As the story goes, her late husband's uncle, George Ross, along with General Washington and Robert Morris were supposed to have been appointed by Congress to design a flag. These gentlemen commissioned Mrs. Ross, a seamstress and an upholsterer, to make the first flag with its thirteen stars and thirteen stripes.

This version of the making of the first Stars and Stripes comes from William J. Canby, a grandson of Mrs. Ross. In 1870, almost a century after the event, he read a paper about the American flag before the Pennsylvania Historical Society first relating these particulars.

None of the authentic records of history substantiate this story. Neither the annals of the Continental Congress nor the personal writings of anyone, including General Washington, shed any light on the question of when, where, or by whom the first American flag was made.

However, we do know that Betsy Ross was paid fourteen pounds twelve shillings and twopence for making ships' colors in May 1777 by the Pennsylvania State Naval Board.

Born in the midst of battle, the first Stars and Stripes proudly announced to the world the birth of a new nation. Slowly it was seen on more and more of the brave American ships that began the commerce which was to make the United States a great power. On land the red, white, and blue banner was borne to the edges of a constantly moving frontier. However, obscure its exact origins, the flag was soon hailed universally as the chief symbol of the Land of the Free.

The First Stars and Stripes, 13 Stars — 13 Stripes
1777-1795

Adopted on June 14, 1777, our first Stars and Stripes contained thirteen stripes, alternating red and white, and thirteen white stars on a field of blue. The stars were arranged in various ways, including the design of the famous Bennington banner (shown here),carried on August 16, 1777 at the Battle of Bennington, just over the Vermont

Famous
Bennington Banner

The 13 Colonies, 1777

N.H.
MASS.
NEW
YORK
R.I.
CONN.
PA.
N.J.
DEL.
VIRGINIA
MARYLAND
NORTH CAROLINA
SOUTH CAROLINA
GEORGIA

border in New York State. Many authorities believe that this banner is the oldest known version of the Stars and Stripes.

The most common variations of the star pattern were a circle of twelve stars with one star in the center or 5 rows of three and two stars alternating. The form bearing 13 stars in a circle was very rarely used at the time. It has become well known largely because artists of the 19th century used it on their paintings.

The States represented by the 13 stars and 13 stripes were the original colonies:

Connecticut, Delaware, Georgia, Maryland, Massachusetts,
New Hampshire, New Jersey, New York, North Carolina,
Pennsylvania, Rhode Island, South Carolina, and Virginia.

The Star Spangled Banner, 15 Stripes
1795-1818

In 1791 Vermont joined the United States and Kentucky followed the next year. Therefore, Congress on January 12, 1794, enacted this law:

"That from and after the first day of May 1795, the Flag of the United States be fifteen stripes, alternate red and white; and that the union be fifteen stars, white, in a blue field."

This is the flag that flew over Fort McHenry, Md., during the bombardment of September 13-14, 1814, and inspired Francis Scott Key to write "The Star-Spangled Banner." It is the only official national flag of the United States with other than 13 stripes.

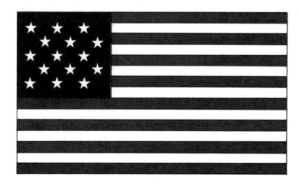

The Star-Spangled Banner

The man who wrote the words to our National Anthem, Francis Scott Key, was a lawyer by profession. He was born in Frederick County, Md., August 1, 1779. He died in Baltimore, Md., on January 11, 1843 and is buried in Frederick. The Star-Spangled Banner he so loved flies day and night over his grave.

During the latter part of August, 1814, Dr. William Beans, a personal friend of Francis Scott Key, was captured by the British Army. Key, living in Baltimore at the time, wrote his mother, saying he was going to plead with the British General Ross to release Dr. Beans.

Proceeding to Chesapeake Bay where the English fleet was massed, Key was kindly received by the British Admiral Cochrane. Because the enemy was prepared to make a combined attack by land and sea on Fort McHenry, General Ross, while consenting to release Dr. Beans, refused to do so immediately, stipulating that every member of the American party would be obliged to remain on the English ship *Surprise* until Fort McHenry was reduced to ashes or captured.

The British fleet poured a blazing shower of shells upon the fortress all during this eventful night, the 13th of September, 1814. Standing at the rail of the English battleship during the terrific bombardment, Key could see from time to time by the glare of the rockets and flashes of the cannon that the American flag was still waving triumphantly over the fort.

During this supreme moment "at the dawn's early light," with the Stars and Stripes still waving triumphantly, Francis Scott Key penned those immortal words. The music which was adopted for The Star-Spangled Banner is taken from an old English song, entitled "To Anacreon in Heaven."

Our National Anthem was first sung in a small one-story house next to a theatre on Holiday Street in Baltimore, Md. Occupied by a Captain MacCauley, it was used by actors who "most did congregate" to prepare themselves for their daily military drill. During these times, every male was a soldier. Ferdinand Durang, a soldier, it is reliably reported, stood on a delapidated chair and for the first time sang this beautiful song. Everyone in attendance joined in at times.

Three copies of the "Star-Spangled Banner" by Francis Scott Key are known to exist. The Library of Congress and the Pennsylvania Historical Society each is in possession of one. Judge J. H. Nicholson, Key's brother-in-law, was given the third. For ninety-three years it remained in the Nicholson family until they sold it in 1907 to Henry Walters of Baltimore, Md. It was purchased in 1934 from the Walters estate and then sold to the Maryland Historical Society.

Our National Anthem

Oh, say, can you see by the dawn's early light,
    What so proudly we hailed at the twilight's last gleaming?
Whose broad stripes and bright stars thro' the perilous fight,
    O'er the ramparts we watched were so gallantly streaming.
And the rockets' red glare, the bombs bursting in air,
    Gave proof through the night that our flag was still there.
Oh, say, does that star-spangled banner yet wave,
O'er the land of the free and the home of the brave?

On the shore dimly seen, thro' the mists of the deep
    Where the foe's haughty host in dread silence reposes,
What is that which the breeze o'er the towering steep,
    As it fitfully blows, half conceals, half discloses?
Now it catches the gleam of the morning's first beam,
    In full glory reflected, now shines on the stream,
'Tis the star-spangled banner, oh, long may it wave
O'er the land of the free and the home of the brave.

Oh, thus be it ever when free men shall stand,
    Between their loved homes and the war's desolation
Blest with vic'try and peace, may the heav'n-rescued land
    Praise the Power that has made and preserved us a nation.
Then conquer we must, when our cause it is just,
    And this be our motto "In God is our trust"
And the star-spangled banner in triumph shall wave
O'er the land of the free and the home of the brave.

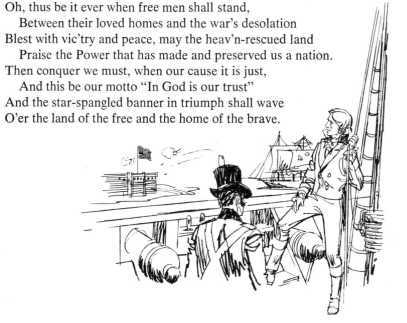

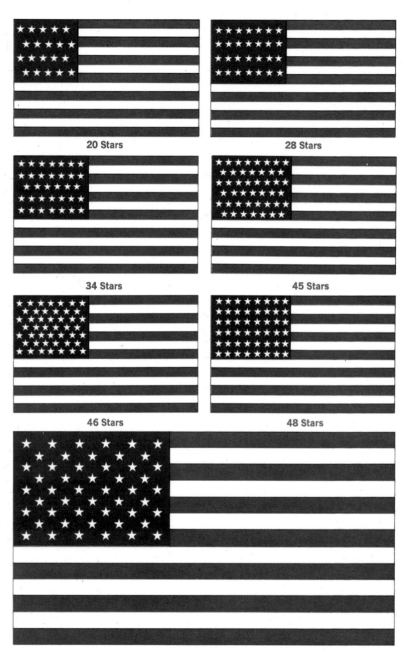

20 Stars

28 Stars

34 Stars

45 Stars

46 Stars

48 Stars

50 Stars

"A Star for Every State" Act, 20 Stars
1818-1819

Realizing that the addition of stripes would make a very complicated flag, Representative Peter Wendover of New York proposed going back to 13 stripes, while continuing to add stars for new States.

An Act of Congress, dated April 4, 1818 reads:

"Be it enacted, That from and after the fourth day of July next, the flag of the United States be thirteen horizontal stripes, alternated red and white; that the union have twenty stars, white in a blue field. And be it further enacted, That on the admission of every new State into the Union, one star be added to the union of the flag; and that such addition shall take effect on the fourth of July next succeeding such admission."

The twenty stars symbolized the admission of the new States of Tennessee (1796), Ohio (1803), Louisiana (1812), Indiana (1816), and Mississippi (1817).

The Mexican War, 28 Stars
1846-1847

When war was declared against Mexico in 1846, there were twenty-eight stars in the union of the American flag. They were sometimes arranged in four rows of seven each. However, like most patterns of the national flag in the 19th century, many variations existed in the arrangement of the stars.

Admitted to the Union since the 20-star flag were Illinois (1818), Alabama (1819), Maine (1820), Missouri (1821), Arkansas (1836), Michigan (1837), Florida (1845), and Texas (1845).

The Eve of the Civil War, 34 Stars
1847-1896

From the beginning of the Mexican War until the start of the Civil War, six more states were admitted to the Union: Iowa (1846), Wisconsin (1848), California (1850), Minnesota (1858), Oregon (1859), and Kansas (1861). In 1861 there were thirty-four stars in the flag. When Southern States seceded from the Union some suggested that their stars be omitted from the flag. But President Lincoln was determined to save the Union intact and refused to allow any change in the flag. Often the Stars and Stripes carried by troops in the Civil War had stars of gold. By 1865 two new stars had been added for West Virginia (1863) and Nevada (1864).

Old Glory, 45 Stars
1896-1908

From the time that General Lee surrendered to General Grant at Appomattox, April 9, 1865, to the declaration of war against Spain on April 18, 1898, nine more states were admitted to the Union, making a total of forty-five stars on the flag. They were usually arranged in six horizontal rows, alternating rows of eight stars each and of seven stars each.

This flag symbolizing a national expansion westward, included stars for the new States of Nebraska (1867), Colorado (1876), Montana (1889), North Dakota (1889), South Dakota (1889), Washington (1889), Wyoming (1890), and Utah (1896).

Old Glory, 46 Stars
1908-1912

In 1908 a forty-sixth star was added to the flag for Oklahoma.

Old Glory, 48 Stars
1912-1959

The design of the 48-star flag was the result of an Executive Order issued by President Taft on June 24, 1912, in which the relative proportions of the flag and the arrangement of the stars were officially prescribed. The stars were arranged in six horizontal rows with eight stars in each row.

This flag represented the completion of the contiguous States of the nation, Arizona and New Mexico having become States in 1912. It would be 47 years, the longest any star design has been in use for a United States flag, before the Stars and Stripes was again modified.

50 Stars
1960 to Present

In 1959 Alaska, separated by Canada from the rest of the States on the North American Continent, joined the Union. A new flag of 49 stars was broken out in its honor. But shortly the insular territory of Hawaii also achieved statehood. The very next year, therefore, our present flag was hoisted. It shows 50 stars arranged in nine horizontal rows of alternately six and five stars.

The growth of our national flag expresses the development of the nation itself. From a small strip of territory along the Atlantic coast, the United States has grown to a huge country which stretches from ocean to ocean. The design of our national banner symbolizes, as it always has, the great diversity of peoples, races, languages, religions and interests which are united in a common nation and destiny.

Origin of the Name
"Old Glory"

The flag of the United States was, at the time of its creation, one of the very few in the world containing stars and stripes. It is not surprising that it acquired the nicknames "the Stars and Stripes" and "the Star-Spangled Banner" many decades ago.

Old Glory as a name for the flag is an altogether different tale. At first it was a single flag that bore the name now familiar to all. The flag belonged to Capt. William Driver.

Driver had received this beautiful American flag in 1831. At that time he was about to sail from his home port of Salem, Massachusetts, on one of the trips he took around the world. The flag went with him on the *Charles Doggett,* his ship, wherever he went.

After countless voyages Capt. Driver retired from the sea and went to live in Nashville, Tennessee. Of course he took Old Glory with him and continued to display it on holidays such as Washington's Birthday, the 4th of July, and St. Patrick's Day (March 17, his own birthday as well). He and his flag became well known in Nashville.

When the Civil War broke out those who hoisted American flags in Nashville were attacked by Southern sympathizers. Confederate soldiers searched Driver's house several times for Old Glory, but never found it. When Union forces entered the city, however, Driver ripped open a bedspread and revealed his flag which had escaped any harm. Seeing it float from the top of the Capitol building in Nashville, Driver declared that he was ready to "meet his forefathers," knowing that Old Glory and Tennessee had been saved for the Union.

After the war the story of Capt. Driver's flag and its name spread by world of mouth and in books and newspapers. Although there is doubt about what eventually became of the original Old Glory, its name lives on in the hearts of millions of Americans.

American Made Flag Material

No one in America, during Colonial times had the "know how" or machinery to produce flag bunting. For almost ninety years American flags were made out of bunting manufactured abroad and were hand stitched.

The Secretary of War commissioned General Benjamin F. Butler to produce a good article of bunting, and a man was sent to England to learn the process. Congress, then (1865) imposed a 40% duty on bunting, affording protection to American manufacturers. Within a few years many American looms were producing fine quality bunting.

It was not until February 1866 that an American made flag was flown over the Capitol in Washington.

Flags on Display

Smithsonian Institute

Among the articles of history contained in the Smithsonian Institute, Washington, D.C., is the flag of Fort McHenry "whose broad stripes and bright stars" inspired Francis Scott Key to write "The Star Spangled Banner." Although still in a tolerable state of preservation, about one-quarter of its original 42-by-30 feet size has been nibbled away by deterioration. Mrs. Mary Pickergill of Baltimore, Md., is credited with having made it.

U.S. Naval Academy

An interesting and historic display of flags and standards is preserved in the Naval Museum at the Naval Academy of Annapolis, Md. Included is the famous "Don't Give Up the Ship" flag flown by Commodore Perry in his noted victory over the British fleet on Lake Erie, September 10, 1813.

West Point Museum

The largest collection of military flags in America is on display in the West Point Museum, West Point, N.Y. About one-third of the seven hundred flags on display are Stars and Stripes. The priceless collection includes a small, two-by-three inch piece of red bunting from the flag lowered at Corregidor after five months of defying the Japanese.

Flag Research Center

In the library and files of the Flag Research Center in Lexington, Massachusetts, will be found the largest existing collection of books, papers, and other materials concerned with flags of the United States. The Center issues a quarterly magazine and many other publications and answers questions concerning flag history and etiquette.

Flags of the Confederacy

The Stars and Bars

The official flags established by the Confederacy during the Civil War included the colors red, white, and blue as well as stars and stripes.

The first flag of the Confederacy, proposed on March 4, 1861 but never officially adopted, consisted of three stripes, alternate red and white, and a square canton of blue containing seven white five-pointed stars in a circle. One star was added for each new State that joined the rebellion until there were 13 in all. This flag was known as the Stars and Bars.

In September, 1861, the "Southern Cross" or Confederate Battle Flag was introduced by three Confederate generals. It consisted of a square field of red with a saltire (diagonal cross) of blue bearing thirteen white five-pointed stars on the arms of the cross. The saltire and the flag both were bordered in white. The flag was never adopted officially, but became popular because of its contrast to the Stars and Stripes.

The Confederate Congress formally adopted its first national flag in April, 1863. This had a white field with the Battle Flag as a canton. Thirteen stars remained on the cross because the South recognized Kentucky and Missouri as Confederate States.

Because the 1863 flag was difficult to distinguish from a white flag of truce when its red and blue canton hung lifeless from a staff, an act of The Confederate Congress on March 4, 1865, ordered an alteration in the form of a red vertical stripe on the outer half of the flag. This flag was barely introduced when the Confederacy ended in April 1865.

The Confederate States of America:

South Carolina, Mississippi, Florida, Alabama, Georgia, Louisiana, Texas, Virginia, Arkansas, North Carolina, Tennessee, Kentucky and Missouri.

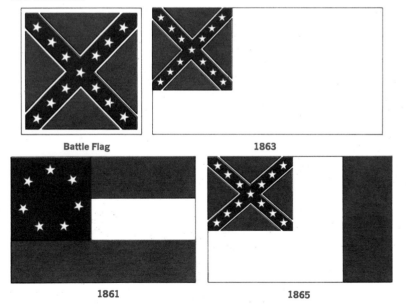

Battle Flag   1863

1861   1865

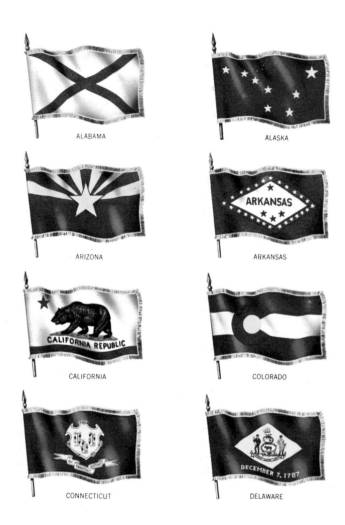

ALABAMA

ALASKA

ARIZONA

ARKANSAS

CALIFORNIA

COLORADO

CONNECTICUT

DELAWARE

FLORIDA

GEORGIA

HAWAII

IDAHO

ILLINOIS

INDIANA

IOWA

KANSAS

KENTUCKY

LOUISIANA

MAINE

MARYLAND

MASSACHUSETTS

MICHIGAN

MINNESOTA

MISSISSIPPI

MISSOURI

MONTANA

NEBRASKA

NEVADA

NEW HAMPSHIRE

NEW JERSEY

NEW MEXICO

NEW YORK

NORTH CAROLINA

NORTH DAKOTA

OHIO

OKLAHOMA

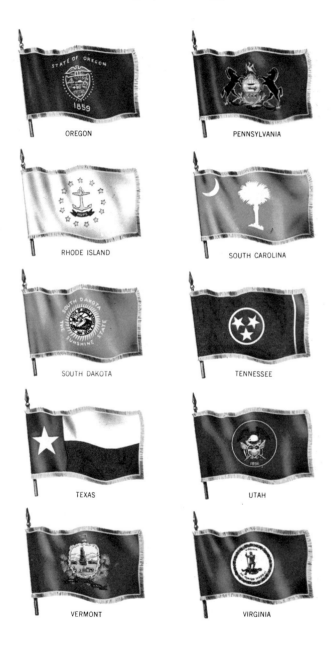

OREGON

PENNSYLVANIA

RHODE ISLAND

SOUTH CAROLINA

SOUTH DAKOTA

TENNESSEE

TEXAS

UTAH

VERMONT

VIRGINIA

Flags of the 50 States

WASHINGTON

WEST VIRGINIA

WISCONSIN

WYOMING

Flags of the Territories

DISTRICT of COLUMBIA

GUAM

PUERTO RICO

VIRGIN ISLANDS

The President's and the Armed Services' Flags

The flag of the President of the United States is a dark blue, rectangular background on which appears the coat-of-arms of the President in proper colors. Basically this is the same as the national arms, the chief difference being the addition of a circle of 50 stars.

The President's Flag

U.S. Army

U.S. Navy

U.S. Marine Corp

U.S. Air Force

U. S. Coast Guard

Flag Day Legalized in 1915

Inspired by the cataclysm of World War I President Woodrow Wilson in 1915, established June 14th as national Flag Day. He said:

"My fellow countrymen: Many circumstances have recently conspired to turn our thoughts to a critical examination of the conditions of our national life, of the influences which have seemed to threaten to divide us in interest and sympathy, of forces within and forces without that seemed likely to draw us away from the happy traditions of united purposes and action of which we have been so proud.

"It has therefore seemed to me fitting that I should call your attention to the approach of the anniversary of the day upon which the Flag of the United States was adopted by the Congress as the emblem of the Union.

"I, therefore, suggest and request that throughout the Nation, and, if possible, in every community, the fourteenth day of June be observed as Flag Day.

"Let us on that day rededicate ourselves to the Nation 'one and inseparable,' from which every thought that is unworthy of our forefathers' first vows of independence, liberty, and right shall be excluded, and in which we shall stand with united hearts for an America which no man can corrupt, no influence draw away from its ideals, no force divide against itself, a nation signally distinguished among all the nations of mankind for its clear, individual conception alike of its duties and its privileges, its obligations, and its rights."

Two of the Largest Flags Ever Made

One of the largest flags ever put together in the United States was made in the 1890's by Miss Josephine Mulford of Madison, N.J. The flag was 100-by-65 feet. The blue field was 40-by-35 feet. Each of the 45 stars measured two feet eight inches across. The stripes were five feet wide. The flag contained as many stitches as there were soldiers in the Spanish-American War — 325,000.

Miss Mulford made five of the stars in the historic places of the states they represent. The Pennsylvania star was made in Philadelphia, partly in the house of Betsy Ross, partly in Carpenter Hall, in the room where the first Continental Congress met, and partly while sitting in John Hancock's chair at Independence Hall, which he occupied when he signed the Declaration of Independence.

The largest United States flag now in use measures 104 feet wide by 235 feet long. Each star is 6 feet tall, while the stripes are 8 feet wide. This banner, which weighs ¾ of a ton is owned by the J. L. Hudson Company in Detroit and is flown every year on Flag Day.

Do's and Don'ts
About The American Flag

☆ Until recently it has been universal custom to display the flag only from sunrise to sunset outdoors. Now however, it is frequent for the flag to be flown day and night, weather permitting. If displayed at night, the flag should be spotlit.

☆ The flag should be hoisted briskly and lowered ceremoniously.

☆ The flag should be displayed daily, weather permitting, on or near the main administration building of every public institution; during school days in or near every schoolhouse, and in or near every polling place on election days.

☆ The flag should be displayed on homes and businesses on all days when the weather permits, especially on national and state holidays and such days as may be proclaimed by the President of the United States. On Memorial Day the flag should be half-staffed until noon.

☆ No disrespect should be shown to the Flag of the United States of America.

☆ The flag should not be dipped to any person or thing. Regimental colors, state flags, and organization or institutional flags are to be dipped as a mark of honor.

☆ The flag should never be displayed with the union down, save as a signal of dire distress.

☆ The flag should never touch anything beneath it, such as the ground, the floor, water, or merchandise.

☆ The flag should never be carried flat or horizontally, but always aloft and free.

☆ The flag should never be used as drapery of any sort whatsoever, never festooned, drawn back, not up, in fold, but always allowed to fall free. Bunting of blue, white, and red, always arranged with the blue above, the white in the middle, and the red below, should be used for covering a speaker's desk, draping the front of a platform, and for decoration in general.

☆ The flag should never be fastened, displayed, used, or stored in such a manner as will permit it to be easily torn, soiled, or damaged in any way.

☆ The flag should never be used as a covering for a ceiling.

☆ The flag should never have placed upon it, nor on any part of it, nor attached to it, any mark, insignia, letter, word, figure, design, picture, or drawing of any nature.

☆ The flag should never be used as a receptacle for receiving, holding, carrying, or delivering anything.

☆ The flag should never be used for advertising purposes in any manner whatsoever. It should not be embroidered on such articles as cushions or handkerchiefs and the like, printed or otherwise impressed on paper napkins or boxes or anything that is designed for temporary use and discard; or used as any portion of a costume or athletic uniform. Advertising signs should not be fastened to a staff or halyard from which the flag is flown.

☆ The flag, when it is in such condition that it is no longer a fitting emblem for display, should be destroyed in a dignified way, preferably by burning.

☆ A Federal law provides that a trademark cannot be registered which consists of or comprises among other things "the flag, coat-of-arms, or other insignia of the United States or any simulation thereof." (Based on Public Law 829 — 77th Congress). In 1968 Congress passed a law imposing up to one year in jail or a $1,000 fine or both for desecrating the flag.

The Growth of the Union

It is popularly believed that each star in the union of the flag represents an individual state. In fact the stars symbolize the states collectively; no particular star "belongs" to any particular state. This is true because there were stars in the American flag before the adoption of a Federal Constitution and the creation of the United States itself.

Dates of Ratification of the Constitution

1 — Delaware
Dec. 7, 1787

2 — Pennsylvania
Dec. 12, 1787

3 — New Jersey
Dec. 18, 1787

4 — Georgia
Jan. 2, 1788

5 — Connecticut
Jan. 9, 1788

6 — Massachusetts
Feb. 6, 1788

7 — Maryland
April 28, 1788

8 — South Carolina
May 23, 1788

9 — New Hampshire
June 21, 1788

10 — Virginia
June 25, 1788

11 — New York
July 26, 1788

12 — North Carolina
Nov. 21, 1789

13 — Rhode Island
May 29, 1790

DATES OF ADMISSION TO THE UNION

14 — Vermont
March 4, 1791

15 — Kentucky
June 1, 1792

16 — Tennessee
June 1, 1796

17 — Ohio
March 1, 1803

18 — Louisiana
April 30, 1812

19 — Indiana
Dec. 11, 1816

20 — Mississippi
Dec. 10, 1817

21 — Illinois
Dec. 3, 1818

22 — Alabama
Dec. 14, 1819

23 — Maine
March 15, 1820

24 — Missouri
Aug. 10, 1821

25 — Arkansas
June 15, 1836

26 — Michigan
Jan. 26, 1837

27 — Florida
March 3, 1845

28 — Texas
Dec. 29, 1845

29 — Iowa
Dec. 28, 1846

30 — Wisconsin
May 29, 1848

31 — California
Sept. 8, 1850

32 — Minnesota
May 11, 1858

33 — Oregon
Feb. 14, 1859

34 — Kansas
Jan. 29, 1861

35 — West Virginia
June 20, 1863

36 — Nevada
Oct. 31, 1864

37 — Nebraska
March 1, 1867

38 — Colorado
Aug. 1, 1876

39 — North Dakota
Nov. 2, 1889

40 — South Dakota
Nov. 2, 1889

41 — Montana
Nov. 8, 1889

42 — Washington
Nov. 11, 1889

43 — Idaho
July 3, 1890

44 — Wyoming
July 10, 1890

45 — Utah
Jan. 4, 1896

46 — Oklahoma
Nov. 16, 1907

47 — New Mexico
Jan. 6, 1912

48 — Arizona
Feb. 14, 1912

49 — Alaska
Jan. 3, 1959

50 — Hawaii
Aug. 21, 1959

Presidents of the United States

No.	Name	Native State	Born	Inaugurated and Served	Died
1. —	George Washington	Va.	1732	1789-1797	1799
2. —	John Adams	Mass.	1735	1797-1801	1826
3. —	Thomas Jefferson	Va.	1743	1801-1809	1826
4. —	James Madison	Va.	1751	1809-1817	1836
5. —	James Monroe	Va.	1758	1817-1825	1831
6. —	John Quincy Adams	Mass	1767	1825-1829	1848
7. —	Andrew Jackson	S.C.	1767	1829-1837	1845
8. —	Martin Van Buren	N.Y.	1782	1837-1841	1862
9. —	William H. Harrison	Va.	1773	1841-1841	1841
10. —	John Tyler	Va.	1790	1841-1845	1862
11. —	James K. Polk	N.C.	1795	1845-1849	1849
12. —	Zachary Taylor	Va.	1784	1849-1850	1850
13. —	Millard Fillmore	N.Y.	1800	1850-1853	1874
14. —	Franklin Pierce	N.H.	1804	1853-1857	1869
15. —	James Buchanan	Penn.	1791	1857-1861	1868
16. —	Abraham Lincoln	Ky.	1809	1861-1865	1865
17. —	Andrew Johnson	N.C.	1808	1865-1869	1875
18. —	Ulysses S. Grant	Ohio	1822	1869-1877	1885
19. —	Rutherford B. Hayes	Ohio	1822	1877-1881	1893
20. —	James A. Garfield	Ohio	1831	1881-1881	1881
21. —	Chester A. Arthur	Vt.	1830	1881-1885	1886
22. —	Grover Cleveland	N.J.	1837	1885-1889	1908
23. —	Benjamin Harrison	Ohio	1833	1889-1893	1901
24. —	Grover Cleveland	N.J.	1837	1893-1897	1908
25. —	William McKinley	Ohio	1843	1897-1901	1901
26. —	Theodore Roosevelt	N.Y.	1858	1901-1909	1919
27. —	William H. Taft	Ohio	1857	1909-1913	1930
28. —	Woodrow Wilson	Va.	1856	1913-1921	1924
29. —	Warren G. Harding	Ohio	1865	1921-1923	1923
30. —	Calvin Coolidge	Vt.	1872	1923-1929	1933
31. —	Herbert Clark Hoover	Iowa	1874	1929-1933	1964
32. —	Franklin D. Roosevelt	N.Y.	1882	1933-1945	1945
33. —	Harry S. Truman	Mo.	1884	1945-1953	
34. —	Dwight D. Eisenhower	Texas	1890	1953-1961	1969
35. —	John F. Kennedy	Mass.	1917	1961-1963	1963
36. —	Lyndon B. Johnson	Texas	1908	1963-1969	
37. —	Richard M. Nixon	Calif.	1913	1969-	

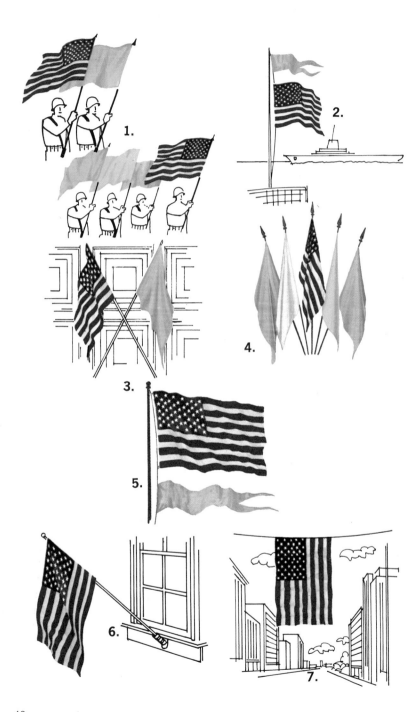

1.

2.

3.

4.

5.

6.

7.

How to Display
the Flag of the United States

1. The flag, when carried in a procession with another flag or flags, should be either on the marching right; that is, the flag's own right, or, if there is a line of other flags, in front of the center of that line. The flag should not be displayed on a float in a parade except from a staff, or so suspended that its folds fall as free as though the flag were staffed.

2. No other flag or pennant should be placed above or, if on the same level, to the right of the flag of the United States of America except during church services conducted by naval chaplains at sea, when the church pennant may be flown above the flag during church services for the personnel of the Navy.

3. The flag of the United States of America, when it is displayed with another flag against a wall from crossed staffs, should be on the right, the flag's own right, and its staff should be in front of the staff of the other flag.

4. The flag of the United States of America should be at the center and at the highest point of the group, when a number of flags of States or localities or pennants of societies are grouped and displayed from staffs.

5. When flags of States, cities, or localities, or pennants of societies are flown on the same halyard with the flag of the United States, the latter should always be at the peak. When the flags are flown from adjacent staffs, the flag of the United States should be hoisted first and lowered last. No such flag or pennant may be placed above the flag of the United States or to the right of the flag of the United States.

6. When the flag of the United States is displayed from a staff projecting horizontally or at any angle from the window sill, balcony, or front of a building, the union of the flag should be placed at the peak of the staff unless the flag is at half staff. When the flag is suspended over a sidewalk from a rope extending from a house to a pole at the edge of the sidewalk, the flag should be hoisted out, union first, from the building.

7. When the flag is displayed otherwise than by being flown from a staff, it should be displayed flat, whether indoors or out, or so suspended that its folds fall as free as though the flag were staffed. When the flag is displayed over the middle of the street, it should be suspended vertically with the union to the north in an east and west street or the east in a north and south street.

8.

9.

10.

11.

12.

13.

14.

8. The flag should form a distinctive feature of the ceremony of unveiling a statue or monument, but it should never be used as the covering for the statue or monument.

9. When the flag is used to cover a casket, it should be so placed that the union is at the head and over the left shoulder. The flag should not be lowered into the grave or allowed to touch the ground. The flag, when flown at half staff, should be first hoisted to the peak for an instant and then lowered to the half-staff position. The flag should be again raised to the peak before it is lowered for the day.

10. During the ceremony of hoisting or lowering the flag or when the flag is passing in a parade, all persons present should face the flag, stand at attention, and salute. Men should remove the headdress, holding it over the heart with the right hand. Men without hats, and women, should salute by placing the right hand over the heart. The salute to the flag in the moving column should be rendered at the moment the flag passes.

11. When the national anthem is played and the flag is not displayed, all present should stand and face toward the music. Those in uniform should salute at the first note of the anthem, retaining this position until the last note. All others should stand at attention, men removing the headdress. When the flag is displayed, all present should face the flag and salute.

12. The pledge of allegiance to the flag, "I pledge allegiance to the flag of the United States of America and to the Republic for which it stands, one Nation under God, indivisible, with liberty and justice for all," should be rendered by standing with the right hand over the heart. Persons in uniform shall render the military salute.

13. When displayed from a staff in a chancel of a church, or on the speaker's platform in a public auditorium, the flag should occupy the position of honor and be placed at the speaker's right. Any other flag on the platform should be placed at the speaker's left, as he faces the audience. But when the flag is displayed elsewhere than on the platform it shall be placed at the right of the audience as they face the platform. Any other flag so displayed should be placed on the left of the audience as they face the platform.

14. When used on a speaker's platform, the flag, if displayed flat, should be displayed above and behind the speaker. The flag may be horizontal or vertical, with the union or field uppermost and to the observers left.

Old Glory on Iwo Jima

The most famous photograph of Old Glory is undoubtedly the one taken by a press photographer of a Marine patrol (Feb. 23, 1945) planting Old Glory on the summit of Mt. Suribachi on Iwo Jima, a volcanic island 650 miles south of Japan in the Pacific during World War II. It was a 96″ x 56″ 48 star flag attached to a Japanese iron pipe. Old Glory has flown continuously on Iwo Jima night and day, rain or shine since that eventful day in February 1945.

The U.S. Marine Corp has immortalized this event in their War Memorial at Arlington, Va. It is the largest bronze statue in the world. Old Glory flies (spotlighted) 24 hours a day in memory of their great victory which cost the lives of over 8000 U.S. men, most of them members of the United States Marine Corp.

Old Glory the First Flag on the Moon

This photograph taken February 5, 1971 by Astronaut Edgar D. Mitchell shows Astronaut Alan B. Shepard Jr., Commander of *Apollo 14* making the third implanting of Old Glory on the surface of the moon. The first was made by Astronauts Neil A. Armstrong and Edwin E. Aldrin Jr. on July 20, 1969 and the second by Astronauts Charles Conrad Jr. and Alan L. Bean on Nov. 19, 1969. All six of these Astronauts were once Scouts. Truly it can be said today, "There isn't a man on this earth who has been on the moon who wasn't first a Boy Scout."

Of the 57 living astronauts 44 were Scouts.

And of the hundreds and hundreds of flags in this world "Old Glory" is the first and only flag on the moon.

About Scouting

In 61 years the Boy Scouts of America has become the largest youth organization of the free world. Presently one out of four boys is a member of the Boy Scouts of America. With the Theme *America's Manpower Begins with BOYPOWER,* the Boy Scouts of America plans by the 200th anniversary of the Nation in 1976 to involve a representative one-third of all boys in a quality Scouting program.

Scouting units are in every nook and cranny of the U.S.A. Currently there are 60,784 Cub packs, 71,655 Scout troops and 23,306 Explorer posts. These 157,116 local units have a total youth membership of 4,682,658. And when the 1,604,626 adult volunteers in Scouting are added, the movement is 6,287,284 strong.

Cub Scouting is a family — and home-centered program for boys who are in the third grade or 8, 9 and 10 years old. Boy Scouting is program for boys in the fifth grade or 11 through 17. Exploring is a contemporary program for high-school-age young men and women that is designed to meet the needs, desires and concerns of the next generation of citizens.

Scouting must have the largest alumni membership of any educational group in America. More than 49,628,050 have been enrolled in its 61-year history!

"This flag, which we honor and under which we serve, is the emblem of our unity, our power, our thought and purpose as a nation. It has no other character than that which we give it from generation to generation. The choices are ours".

President Woodrow Wilson

Do you fly Old Glory at your house?

*For information on a
beautiful inexpensive flag
with holder and pole
call Boy Scouts of America.
They are listed in
your phone book.*

More About the Flag

Many books, articles, and films have been produced about the history and meaning of the flag of the United States. Many of these include inaccurate information, but many others are excellent sources of information. The best references are the following:

BROAD STRIPES AND BRIGHT STARS (American Heritage, 1970)

Blassingame, Wyatt, THE STORY OF THE UNITED STATES FLAG (Garrard, 1969)

Department of Defense, OUR FLAG (1970 edition)

Moss, J. A., THE FLAG OF THE UNITED STATES (various publishers and editions)

Quaife, M. M., THE FLAG OF THE UNITED STATES (Grosset & Dunlap, 1942)

Quaife, M. M. and others, THE HISTORY OF THE UNITED STATES FLAG (Harper, 1961)

Smith, Whitney, THE FLAG BOOK OF THE UNITED STATES (Morrow, 1970)

"THE UNITED STATES FLAG: LIVING SYMBOL OF OUR HISTORY" (Scott, Foresman: 1970; a filmstrip)